PYTHONS

AMAZING SNAKES

Ted O'Hare

Rourke

Publishing LLC

Vero Beach, Florida 32964

www.rourkepublishing.com

PHOTO CREDITS: Title page, pp 9, 11, 22 © James H. Carmichael; pp 4, 6, 8, 10, 15, 16, 18, 20, 21 © Lynn M. Stone; p 12 © George Van Horn; p 17 © Joe McDonald/Bruce Coleman, Inc.

Title Page: *The world's longest snakes are reticulated pythons.*

Editor: Frank Sloan

Cover and interior design by Nicola Stratford

Library of Congress Cataloging-in-Publication Data

O'Hare, Ted, 1961-
  Pythons / Ted O'Hare.
      p. cm. -- (Amazing snakes)
  Includes bibliographical references and index.
  ISBN 1-59515-148-6 (hardcover)
  1. Pythons--Juvenile literature. I. Title. II.Series: O'Hare, Ted, 1961- Amazing snakes.
  QL666.O67O42 2004
  597.96'78--dc22
                              2004008018

Printed in the USA

table of contents

Pythons

The python is a member of the *Pythonidae* family. Like all snakes, pythons are **reptiles**. The python does not contain any **venom**. Instead, it captures its **prey** by **constriction**.

Because they began to live underground, snakes lost their need for legs. Today's python still has parts of its pelvis. This is evidence of its ancestral legs. It also has horny claws where its legs used to be.

Pythons kill prey by gripping it tightly in their coils, which prevents the victim from breathing.

where they Live

Pythons live in Southeastern Asia, the East Indies, Africa, Australia, Central America, and India. Many of these places have tropical climates with heavy rainfall. Some species are found in dry deserts, while others live in mountains. Most pythons live on the ground. Some can climb trees, and most are good swimmers.

The green tree python of New Guinea lives in a wet, tropical habitat.

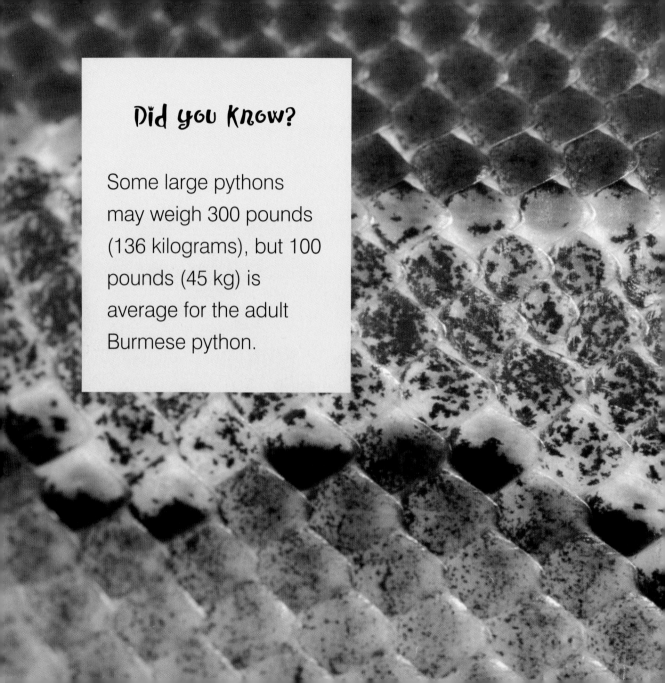

Did You Know?

Some large pythons may weigh 300 pounds (136 kilograms), but 100 pounds (45 kg) is average for the adult Burmese python.

what they Look Like

Pythons' large bodies are covered with smooth, shiny scales. The python moves slowly and quietly. Python colors vary, depending on the **species**. Many have patterns of yellow, brown, gray, white, and black.

The Burmese python of Asia grows to more than 25 feet (7.6 m) in length, making it one of the largest pythons.

The colors of a python's shiny scales vary from one species to another and even within a species!

their senses

A python flicks out its tongue to decide if an object is a suitable meal. The tongue then takes particles to the **Jacobson's organ**. This, along with the snake's **heat receptor pits**, quickly locates the prey.

If the senses know that the prey is near, the kill follows rapidly. This entire process takes only seconds.

The carpet python is related to the diamond python.

An Australian diamond python senses for prey or danger by darting its tongue.

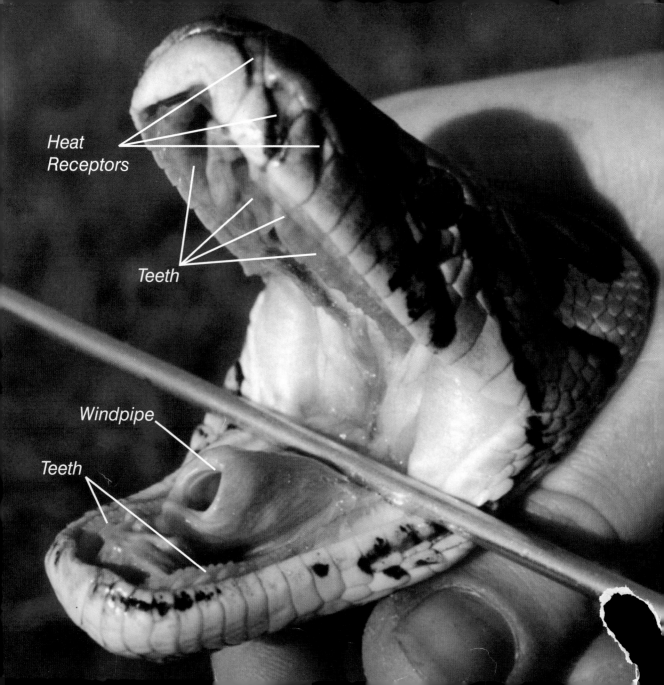

Heat
Receptors

Teeth

Windpipe

Teeth

the Head and Mouth

The python's head has powerful jaw muscles. The heat receptor pits are found around the edges of the upper and lower jaws. Because it is not venomous, the python has no fangs.

Instead the python has long teeth. The teeth are curved inward. This lets the snake get a firm grip on the prey during constriction.

The open mouth of a python shows its sharp teeth.

As the python grips its prey, the victim struggles for freedom. This causes the snake's long, curved teeth to grasp the prey strongly.

Did you know?

Pythons have six rows of teeth. Two rows are in the lower jaw, and four are in the upper jaw.

14

A python grasps the head of its prey while the snake's coils constrict the body.

Baby Pythons

Remaining still among the leaves helps a python hide.

The mother python lays as many as 100 eggs at a time. The mother keeps the eggs warm with her coiled body and also by sunlight. In about two months the eggs hatch.

At birth the baby reticulated python weighs 4 ounces (113 grams) and is about 25 inches (64 centimeters) long.

Newly hatched Burmese pythons crawl over eggs that will themselves soon hatch.

Did you Know?

A large python is
able to swallow prey
weighing as much as
100 pounds (45 kg).

their prey

A python lies in wait to ambush its prey. Then the snake firmly holds it prey. The python coils its body around the prey. Each time the prey breathes, the snake coils tighter. This causes the prey to **suffocate**. This method of killing is known as constriction.

After killing its prey, a python begins to swallow it whole.

their Defense

Pythons are able to avoid enemies because they hide so well. A lot of this has to do with **camouflage**.

When attacked, however, a python fights back intensely. The python grabs the enemy with its long teeth. Then the python rips through the attacker's flesh.

A green tree python waits in silent ambush.

Camouflage helps a python ambush prey and avoid enemies.

index

Further Reading

Weber, Valerie J. *African Rock Pythons*. Gareth Stevens, 2003.
—*Asian Rock Pythons*. Gareth Stevens, 2003.
—*Reticulated Pythons*. Gareth Stevens, 2003.

Websites to Visit

members.aol.com/bigdadyrob/pythons.html
www.enchantedlearning.com/subjects/reptiles/snakes/printouts.shtml
www.42explore.com/snake2.htm

About the Author

Ted O'Hare is an author and editor of children's nonfiction books. He divides his time between New York City and a home upstate.